COPING WITH

ONLINE FLAMING
AND TROLLING

Sherri Mabry Gordon

Rosen
YA™

Published in 2019 by The Rosen Publishing Group, Inc.
29 East 21st Street, New York, NY 10010

Library of Congress Cataloging-in-Publication Data

Names: Gordon, Sherri Mabry, author.
Title: Coping with online flaming and trolling / Sherri Mabry Gordon.
Description: New York : Rosen Publishing, 2019. | Series: Coping | Includes bibliographical references and index. | Audience: Grades 7–12.
Identifiers: LCCN 2017053661| ISBN 9781508179054 (library bound) | ISBN 9781508179047 (pbk.)
Subjects: LCSH: Online etiquette—Juvenile literature. | Online trolling—Juvenile literature. | Internet and teenagers—Juvenile literature.
Classification: LCC TK5105.878 .G67 2019 | DDC 395.5—dc23
LC record available at https://lccn.loc.gov/2017053661

Manufactured in the United States of America

CONTENTS

INTRODUCTION

For well-known sixteen-year-old YouTuber, Brianna Hill, online trolling and hateful comments are to be expected. In fact, any time you put present yourself online in a public way, people see that as an opportunity to troll you, she says.

But Brianna, who publishes the popular YouTube channel BriannaxBeautyx, has learned how to deal with the trolls in a healthy and productive way, although she admits it was not easy at first. Brianna had her first experience with online trolls in seventh grade, after one of her fashion and beauty videos went viral.

She says,

"Once my video went viral I got a lot of hate and I wasn't used to that," "Usually, all of the comments on my videos were positive. But once my videos started reaching a broader audience, people started commenting on how I looked and what I was saying. They would say things like my eyebrows were too 'bushy.' Or they would say 'don't listen to her, she doesn't know what she's talking about.' And at first, I started to wonder if I should even be doing YouTube videos."

She says she even went through a phase where all she would read were the negative comments. "I was hurt and confused," she recalls. "I didn't understand

Trolling often occurs on YouTube. For Brianna Hill, a popular YouTuber, coping with trolls was not easy. But with practice, she learned to deal with them in a healthy way.

why people needed to hide behind a computer screen and put someone else down."

Eventually, she says she got over her fixation on the trolls and started focusing on the positive comments as well as the constructive criticism she received. "There's a difference between hate and criticism," she says. "I realized I needed to ignore the hate and listen to the criticism. The people leaving critical remarks were telling me how I could make my videos better by asking why I didn't include this product or suggesting that I do something differently. But the hate wasn't useful. I just ignored it."

Fortunately, Brianna didn't let the trolling keep her from pursuing her passion. Today, she has more than 100,000 subscribers and her videos are some of the most popular teen-produced fashion and beauty videos online. What's more, she is regularly contacted by companies and brands about reviewing their products and has received countless sponsorship opportunities.

"The best advice I can give is to ignore it and delete it if you can," she says. "Try to focus on the positive instead. And if there are no positive comments, seek help from other people."

Brianna says she found it helpful to confide in people she trusts and tell them how she was feeling.

"When something negative is said about you online, it can make you feel like everyone knows about it," she says. "Instead of bottling up this fear and anxiety, it can make you feel better to get help from supportive people."

CHAPTER ONE

A Closer Look at Flaming and Trolling

When most people think of trolls, they envision the manipulative little creatures from fairytales that live under bridges tricking those passing by into doing their bidding. And while these mythical creatures are not real, there are some real-life trolls that people deal with every day that are just as manipulative. Like the trolls of fairytales, these trolls live in the shadows of the internet and get their entertainment and enjoyment from making people's lives miserable.

Trolls are people who intentionally aggravate others online by posting offensive comments, content, or pictures. When a person attacks another person online for their thoughts, beliefs, opinions, or physical appearance, this is called trolling. Like trolling, flaming involves saying mean things online.

Typically, flaming is a hostile and insulting interaction between people online that usually involves

Cyberbullies use shame, humiliation, and intimidation to damage another person's reputation and social status, and they usually know the person they are targeting.

profanity. These flames, or insults, can be thrown back and forth between several people but they also can involve one person or a group of people teaming up on a single person. What's more, flaming is often a tool that can be used by trolls.

Spot the Differences Between Cyberbullying, Trolling, and Flaming

It is not uncommon for people to confuse cyberbullying, trolling, and flaming. After all, they all consist of mean behavior that is played out online. But while each of these bullies may use the same methods to hurt people, their goals are very different.

For instance, trolls are looking to make a disruption online and will target anyone. Typically, they troll public comment sections, Twitter, YouTube, and public social media pages looking for opportunities. Their goal is to attract attention and a disrupt conversations. The more attention they get, the happier they are. Trolling is entertainment for them. They get enjoyment from creating distractions, making people upset, or hijacking conversations.

Meanwhile, cyberbullying is much more personal. Cyberbullies target specific people with their mean words and hateful comments. Their goals are to shame, humiliate, and intimidate the target in order to damage her reputation and her social status. In the end, cyberbullying is about having power and control over someone. And many times, a cyberbully knows her victim.

Another key distinction between cyberbullies and trolls is how they view their hurtful comments, name-calling, and shaming tactics. In general, trolls do not think about how much their comments and posts hurt other people. Their primary goal is to get a reaction from the online community. They crave the attention, good or bad. And, the more attention they get, the happier they are. Meanwhile, cyberbullies do not want attention for themselves. Instead, they want all the negative attention to be directed at the victim. And their goal is to cause as much pain and humiliation as they can for that person.

Flaming on the other hand can exist on its own or serve as a tactic or tool used by both trolls and cyberbullies. When someone flames another person, he attacks her with hostile words, profanity, and accusations. The attack, or "flame," is usually direct, hurtful, and laced with anger. It is important to remember that not all trolling and cyberbullying involves flaming. Sometimes trolling and cyberbullying is much more covert and planned out. Cyberbullies are looking to damage someone's reputation where a flamer is looking to insult people.

Recognize Trolling and Flaming in Your Life

Trolling is a strange twist of events that often occurs when you least expect it. Not only are you caught off guard, but it can even be frightening if the comments are particularly mean or threatening. The first time you encounter an internet troll can be an overwhelming and confusing experience, says Olivia Buoni, a seventeen-year-old student from central Ohio. It can be hard to make sense of why someone is attacking you.

Suddenly, out of nowhere, someone starts attacking you online, making really hurtful comments, she says. It can be a shock to your system and very overwhelming.

Sometimes trolls will flame you by using filthy language, making wild insults, and creating misrepresentations of what you posted. Here are some ways to identify trolling. Trolls usually do the following:

- **Make personal attacks**. Once a troll has decided to target you, they zero in on you with laser vision. Everything you say or do online suddenly becomes ammunition for their attacks. They also insult and flame you with the goal of making you feel bad.

The goal is to humiliate you and damage your reputation.

- **Lace comments with accusations**. Trolls rely on accusation. They break you down and torture you by turning your words against you. They twist your statements and pound away at every aspect of your viewpoint. No matter what you say, trolls question you as a person. What's more, these accusations make you doubt who you are and cripple your self-confidence.

- **Refuse to say anything nice**. Trolls refuse to compliment you or see good in you. They want to destroy you online. They will never acknowledge the smart things you say or the good things you do. Instead, they will find a way to twist those things and use them against you. Their goal is to humiliate you and use your words against you in order to get attention.

- **Put words in your mouth**. For instance, a troll might start their post with something like: "Nut jobs like you think . . ." Or, they might say, "Stupid people like you only know how to . . ." The point is that they are not only accusing you of something, but they also are making assumptions about what you think, feel, and do. It is a form of character assassination.

Trolls devote large amounts of time to creating disruptions online. They feed on the drama and relish the emotionally charged responses they often get.

- **Refuse to acknowledge the truth.** Even when you, or others online, call out trolls for being wrong or not stating the facts, they will keep on trolling. In fact, the more you or others argue with them, the more enjoyment they get from the interaction. Their goal is not to be right but to inflame and disrupt the conversation.
- **Disregard online rules.** Trolls do not follow the rules for forums or comments. They also do not follow social media guidelines and have no digital etiquette. And, when they get kicked off, they will just come back with a different username. They want to change a serious discussion or lighthearted post into a personal attack.
- **Use foul language.** When trolls resort to flaming, they will use profanity and derogatory language. The goal is to roast you with crude words. There is something very damaging about being spoken about with curse words. It amplifies the attack and makes it more damaging mentally.
- **Fire off posts quickly.** Usually trolls have large amounts of free time. As a result, they enjoy starting fights and creating disruptions online. They feed on the drama and devote large amounts of time to this activity. If you make the mistake of engaging with trolls

online, you will be shocked at how quickly they respond.

Trolling Affects Everyone—Even Bystanders

Research shows that trolling and flaming causes significant emotional and psychological distress. And, just like any other victim of online bullying, teens

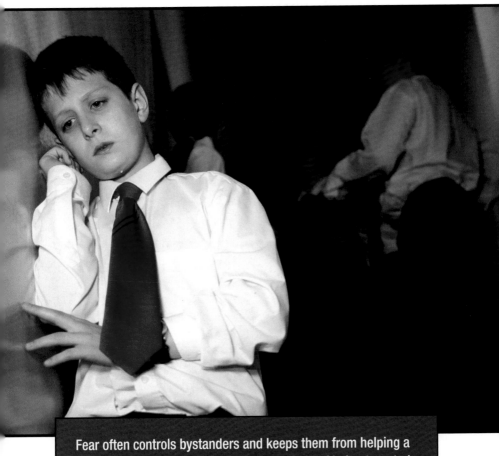

Fear often controls bystanders and keeps them from helping a victim. In fact, bystanders are often so afraid of being targeted by a troll, they refuse to do anything at all.

who are trolled experience anxiety, fear, depression, and low self-esteem. And in extreme cases they may contemplate suicide. In fact, there are multiple cases of teens who were trolled so regularly and so fiercely that they wrongly felt they had no other option.

Even people who are not the target of trolling or flaming are impacted. Yet, less than 20 percent of bystanders will get involved and help a victim of trolling. Here are some emotions bystanders to trolling and flaming might experience:

- *Uncertainty.* Most bystanders see trolling or flaming online and know that it is wrong, but they have no idea what to do.
- *Fear.* Some bystanders fail to do or say anything because they are afraid of being embarrassed or ridiculed just like the victim. They also may fear making the situation worse.
- *Guilt.* Once a bystander watches trolling unfold, they often cannot let the situation go. As a result, they often experience guilt over not stepping in.
- *Anxiety.* After witnessing trolling or flaming online, it is not uncommon for bystanders to develop anxiety. They worry that they will become targets, too. Sometimes in an attempt to cope with anxiety, bystanders will join in trolling as a defense mechanism. They are

worried about becoming a victim as well. So, their goal is to keep the attention on the target and away from them.

Trolling Can Make You Sad

It is normal to feel sad after being trolled. In fact, victims may feel so much grief and sadness that they are not sure how they are going to survive, Olivia says. "But, if you focus on making healthy choices,

Being trolled or flamed online is not easy to deal with. Sometimes victims struggle with anxiety and never want to leave their house.

17

eventually your sadness will lift and you will start to feel normal again."

Sometimes when people are trolled or flamed online, they feel like they are getting sadder every day. They also may struggle with anxiety and not want to leave their house. It is especially worrisome if it starts to affect their day-to-day lives. For instance, if you no longer enjoy your favorite activities, do not have an appetite, and want to sleep all day, you need to talk to someone about what you are experiencing.

This is not normal sadness. In fact, you may be struggling with depression and should talk to your doctor about your symptoms. Do not hide what is happening. You have no reason to feel embarrassed by what you're feeling. With the right treatment, and the healthiest coping mechanisms, you will be back to your old self before you know it.

Myths & FACTS

Myth: When it comes to a troll, fight fire with fire.

Fact: It is almost never a good idea to engage a troll online. Instead, try to ignore the troll. You may want to take a few screenshots of his comments and then block him from your account. The screenshots serve as proof of the trolling you experienced.

Myth: Trolling and cyberbullying are the same thing.

Fact: There are actually a number of differences between trolling and cyberbullying. For instance, trolls want attention, good or bad, while cyberbullies want to focus negative attention on the victim of cyberbullying.

Myth: Only adults are being trolled online.

Fact: While a lot of adults are affected by trolling—especially during an election year or while discussing volatile topics—they are not the only victims. Countless numbers of teens are trolled online every day.

(continued on the next page)

(continued from the previous page)

Myth: Trolling and flaming others is harmless fun.

Fact: While a troll may get enjoyment from what he is doing, it is never fun for the person on the receiving end. In fact, the emotional scars from trolling and flaming can last a lifetime.

Myth: Being trolled or flamed builds character and will make you stronger.

Fact: In no way will trolling and flaming build character. Instead, it tears away at a person's character and increases her vulnerabilities. You can, however, choose to do something positive with the negative experience of trolling and flaming.

Myth: Trolling and flaming are not a big deal; it's just kids being kids.

Fact: Being victimized by trolls is a very big deal. People who are trolled suffer both emotionally and socially. They also feel alone and isolated. They may struggle with low self-esteem, experience depression, and battle thoughts of suicide.

Myth: All trolls are loners and have no friends.

Fact: While some trolls may in fact be loners, there are many different types of trolls out there. And some trolls have large circles of friends and still enjoy making other people upset online.

Myth: Flaming and trolling could never happen to me.

Fact: About one in four Americans have experienced trolling, flaming, or another form of online harassment. What's more, 66 percent of people have witnessed others being trolled. So the probability that you will at least see trolling occur is quite high.

Myth: Trolls have no influence online.

Fact: According to an online study by the National

(continued on the next page)

(continued from the previous page)

Science Foundation, bashing someone online as well as having negative debates can impact a person's credibility, especially if the topics are controversial in nature.

Myth: There is no way to fight back against trolls.

Fact: It is usually not recommended that you engage with a troll or flamer online, but there are other actions you can take. For instance, blocking a troll and reporting her behavior are two very good first steps in dealing with the behavior.

The Effects of Flaming and Trolling

When seventeen-year-old Olivia Buoni was in seventh grade, Instagram was still in its infancy. And like other teens her age, she fell in love with the photo-sharing site. It became another way to share a little bit about herself and to communicate with others in a new and different way.

Developed in 2010, Instagram was an instant hit. And kids like Olivia were just learning how to use the social media platform. As a result, she saw nothing wrong with posting public pictures of herself and sharing her life through photos.

"Instagram was still pretty new back then. So, I thought nothing of putting myself out there," Olivia says. "I expected it to be a lot like talking to friends in real life. But social media makes people brave; and they say things they might never say in person."

Many kids may not realize the risks of sharing photos of their lives on Instagram. They have no idea that trolls exploit photos by posting mean and hurtful comments.

She says she learned the hard way that people are not always who you think they are online. Some of the girls making mean remarks about her went to her school and others were random girls she had never met. "People can change quickly online. One day they are your best friend and the next day they are not," she warns.

"Hiding behind a keyboard makes people do or say things that they may not have the courage to say in person," Olivia says. "I learned very quickly that you cannot post personal things like who you like, what happened to you at school, or ask for honest feedback. People will take that information and use it against you. People can be really mean online."

For Olivia, her issues with trolling and cyberbullying began with a few innocent selfies she took of herself in new outfits. But she was not prepared for the responses she received. People commented on the photos with comments like: "That outfit doesn't look good on you," "That outfit is ugly," "You're ugly," and other hateful things. Another time she reached out online for help with math, but received comments like "You're so stupid."

People even cyberbullied and trolled her about incidents that occurred at school. After a painful bullying incident in the gym locker room, the bully later bragged on social media that she "whooped this little girl in gym class."

"The rude comments really dug into me," she says. "My body image and self-esteem really began to fall because of people tearing into me."

Eventually, the trolling and cyberbullying she experienced online became too much for her. Late one evening, Olivia posted that she wanted to kill herself. Fortunately for her, a classmate saw her post and told her mom. This classmate's mom then found a way to contact Olivia's parents and tell them about her cry for help.

"They came rushing into my room and it really brought me to tears," Olivia recounts. "They didn't know what I was going through. It was really hard to admit what I was experiencing. It is so humiliating to tell another person all the hateful things people are saying about you."

At this point, Olivia was so depressed she could no longer attend school. She worried about what people were thinking and saying about her. And she wondered just how many people knew what the trolls were saying about her online. She felt alone, helpless, and misunderstood.

"My parents pulled me out of school and I was homeschooled for the remainder of seventh grade," she says. "That was hard, too, because I was still alone. But by the fall of my eighth-grade year, they had enrolled me in a private school."

She admits that making new friends was hard at first. She wasn't sure who she could trust. But

Dealing with online trolling and flaming should never be done alone. With the help of parents, teachers, and friends, you can get through the experience and feel confident again.

she says the students at her new school were very open to including her. "I had never experienced what it felt like to be included," she says. "I felt loved and protected at my new school. Having a group of friends that has your back is really important, especially when you are going through something like trolling online."

Today, Olivia says she has learned to accept what happened to her but has not forgotten the lessons she learned. "I knew I couldn't just forget about the trolling and cyberbullying," she says. "It is part of who I am and my testimony. I learned that I am capable of standing back up and I want others to know that they can stand up, too."

She credits her parents and her friends with helping her get through the darkest hours of her experience, but also knows that she would not be where she is today if she had not done some hard work as well.

"I just really needed to grab ahold of that self-confidence again," she explains. "I had to make that choice myself—to pick myself back up and realize I can do this. I can overcome this."

Trolls Leave Bruises on the Inside

Unless you have been victimized by a troll, you will not understand the deep pain, anxiety, confusion, and humiliation that victims of trolling experience. Being trolled is a life-changing experience that affects victims in ways most people just do not realize. From stomachaches and intense anxiety to negative self-image and intense stress, the effects of trolling are extensive. Here are seven things about trolling that victims often say about their experience.

1. *"Trolling messes with your mind."* Being on the receiving end of trolling affects a victim's thoughts and beliefs. For instance, it is not uncommon for victims of trolling to start to believe all the negative things a troll says about them. They may even believe that everyone else agrees with the troll, especially if no one steps in to defend them or say something nice.

2. *"I am not overreacting."* The emotions that trolling stirs up in a person are very real and very intense. Yet, people often downplay or minimize what they are experiencing. But many people do not understand trolling and often question a victim's reaction. It is not uncommon for people to think that a victim is making a bigger issue out of trolling and flaming than they need to.

3. *"Telling me to get over it is not helpful."* It is never a good idea to tell a victim of trolling to calm down or get over it. Victims of trolling need to feel like you understand and that you empathize with what they are experiencing. Try to be patient and understanding when someone has been trolled or flamed online. Listen to what they have to say and validate their feelings.

4. *"Being trolled is making me sick."* The effects of trolling can show up in a number of different

Sometimes trolling makes victims sick. In fact, they can experience everything from depression and anxiety to stomach ulcers, dizziness, and even heart palpitations.

ways. It is not uncommon for teens impacted by trolling to suffer from depression, anxiety, and even thoughts of suicide. Likewise, the stress that trolling causes raise other issues, too. For example, victims might experience everything from dizziness and stomach ulcers to rapid heart rates and panic attacks.

5. *"Being trolled online has changed me."* Research shows that the effects of trolling have a long-lasting impact on victims. In fact, they may struggle with the experience well into adulthood. For this reason, it is critical to be positive and supportive to victims of trolling. They are likely much more sensitive than they used to be.

6. *"I feel hopeless, powerless, and alone."* Trolling is one of the most emotionally damaging experiences someone can go through. Even when he or she is surrounded by friends and family, a victim of trolling can feel very alone. Part of this comes from being powerless to make the trolling stop or go away. The negative messages are out there online, for the entire world to see. Trolling also causes victims to isolate themselves from friends and family. Victims are often too embarrassed to talk with others about what is happening. So, they stop interacting with other people.

7. *"One person's kindness changes everything."* Sometimes all it takes is for one person to say something kind or encouraging to a victim of trolling to truly help him or her. This small step gives the victim a sense of hope that not everyone believes the lies that the troll is spewing.

Suicide Warning Signs

If you or someone you know displays any of these signs after being trolled, contact a trusted adult right away. Or, contact the National Suicide Prevention Lifeline at 800-273-8255. If you or friend does any of these things, you need to get help right away:

- Mentions suicide or says he or she wants to die
- Says that no one cares and that no one would miss him or her after s/he's gone
- Makes comments about feeling hopeless, helpless, or worthless
- Becomes preoccupied with death and dying
- Does things that do not make sense or are out of character
- Refuses to participate in his or her favorite activities
- Isolates himself or herself from others
- Makes risky decisions and takes chances
- Appears self-destructive
- Starts giving away his or her stuff, even things that are really special to him or her
- Writes notes or calls people to tell them how much he or she loves them
- Posts sad or hopeless comments online

Finding Your Way Back After a Troll Attack

Every day, countless teens are dealing with trolling online. But it doesn't have to be the end of the world. There is life after trolling, Olivia says.

"I had to take some time and rediscover who I was," she says. "It is too easy to believe the lies that trolls say about you. But what I learned is that you have to reject those words and learn to appreciate who you are."

Here are some other ideas on how you can feel good about who you are again:

- *Accept that your feelings are normal.* There is nothing wrong with feeling sad, angry, confused, and upset about what happened to you. You are not going crazy. These feelings are a normal response to the stress of trolling and flaming. Just make it a goal not to stay in this place but to instead work to overcome these feelings.
- *Talk to people you trust.* Do not be afraid to reach out to other people and ask for help, Olivia suggests. "I was afraid more people would know if I asked for help," she says. "But don't be afraid to talk about what you're going through. Keeping your feelings inside is not healthy."

When dealing with online trolling, focus on the positive things in your life. Exercise and fresh air are often an important part of healing.

- *Create a technology-free space in your house.* Because trolling happens online, you need to make space for yourself where you can be free of technology for a little bit. Having a dedicated space to do that helps. Pick a space in your room, a special spot outside, or a quiet spot at the library to kick back and relax. Listen to music, read, or write in a journal. All of these things go a long way in helping you cope with the intense feelings that trolling creates.

- *Keep living your life.* A troll wants to disrupt your life. Do not let him steal from you. Continue doing the things you enjoy. Stay involved in activities, hang out with friends, and keep up with your schoolwork. Yes, trolling is awful. But try not to dwell on it. Do not let it negatively impact all the positives in your life.

- *Remember that perceptions can become reality.* Avoid giving the troll too much power in your life. For instance, if you dwell on the humiliation or embarrassment of being trolled or flamed, then you will feel humiliated and embarrassed. But if you think about how you stood up for yourself, blocked the troll, and reported him to the proper authorities, you will feel empowered. Remember that how you view a situation will be how you feel about it, too.

- *Take control of your thoughts.* Remember, your attitude doesn't come from being trolled, but instead from how you interpret being trolled. As a result, take full responsibility for your feelings and your outlook. If you remain positive despite what has happened to you, the trolling will have less of an effect.
- *Focus on healing.* Trolling can do a lot of harm. So, it is important to take care of yourself much in the same way you would if you were recovering from the flu. Be sure to get plenty of rest. Eat nutritious food and try to exercise. All of these things are an important part of the healing process.
- *Put aside victim thinking.* Avoid dwelling on what happened to you. Do not relive it or reread all the mean comments. Doing so keeps you trapped in victim mode. Although you do not have to forget what happened to you, it is important not to let it control your thoughts. Allow yourself a few minutes to grieve over what the troll has done, then tell yourself that you are going to think about something else. Focus on something positive in your life instead.
- *Look for meaning in this experience.* While it is true that what you experienced is horrible, it does not have to define who you are. Instead,

try to think about what you learned. For example, did you learn to be more assertive? Are you more careful about posting online? Did this experience make you stronger? The things you learned from your experience may help someone else in the future.

You Have a Choice

The key to understanding trolling is to recognize that trolls made a choice to target you. You did not deserve to be trolled or flamed; but you have a choice about how you will respond. You cannot allow what happened to you to define who you are as a person. Everyone deserves respect, including you.

That's why you need to place the responsibility for

When trying to make sense of trolling, remember that the troll made a choice to target you. You did not deserve it. Everyone deserves to be treated with kindness and respect.

trolling on the shoulders of the troll and move on. Leave his hurtful words, name-calling, and rudeness in the past. Letting go and moving on is an important part of the healing process.

Always remember, your identity is not tied to the mean and hurtful things the troll said about you. Consequently, do not allow yourself to focus on his behavior. This is what he wants. Instead, make a choice to find healthy ways to focus on who you really are. You are special and important and no troll has a right to diminish that.

CHAPTER THREE

Inside the Minds of People Who Flame or Troll Others

Trolls and flamers are hiding everywhere. They lurk in dark corners and prowl the shadows looking for the perfect opportunity to strike. They read the comment sections of controversial new articles, view YouTube videos, and scan Twitter.

They are hunting for victims who say things they can exploit. It can be something as harmless as a positive tweet about a favorite sports team or something more serious like a display of emotion or feelings online. Regardless of what it is, when they see their opportunity, they will jump on it with full force.

Their weapons consist of everything from foul words, sarcastic remarks, and taunts to memes, threats, and ridicules. While there are a few trolls and flamers who are just looking for a laugh, the majority of them are out to ruin someone's day—just because they can.

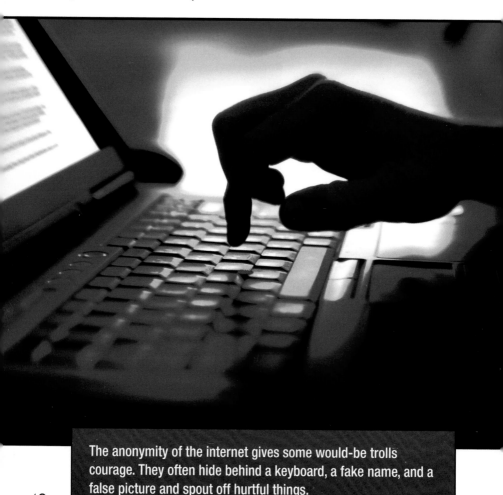

The anonymity of the internet gives some would-be trolls courage. They often hide behind a keyboard, a fake name, and a false picture and spout off hurtful things.

For some trolls, the supposed anonymity of the internet gives them the courage to say things they would never say in person. For others, they are just as cruel in person. Either way, trolls and flamers often hide behind a keyboard, a fake name, and a false picture and spout off whatever hurtful things they can dream up. This secrecy often keeps them from experiencing any consequences for their behavior.

Surprisingly, more people have engaged in trolling and flaming than you might realize. In fact, according to one poll, nearly a quarter of those who have posted online admit to trolling or flaming strangers over an opinion. That being said, there are those people who occasionally troll and flame others and then there are others who do it on a daily basis.

What Makes Them Do It?

Some psychologists believe that habitual trolls and flamers, those who troll others frequently, have characteristics similar to psychopaths. In other words, they do not feel empathy, guilt, remorse, or responsibility for their actions. Additionally, they tend to have sadistic traits as well and enjoy causing other people physical and psychological pain. In short, internet trolls and flamers get a kick out of making other people feel bad.

Trolls and flamers also are motivated by "atypical social rewards," which according to psychologists means they are looking for negative social rewards like social mayhem and disruption. Likewise, they are not interested in positive social rewards like acceptance, popularity, and likability. Their primary goal is to hurt others. And if you let them know you are hurt by their remarks, they get some enjoyment from that.

Research also suggests that trolls and flamers have high levels of cognitive empathy. In other words, they understand people's emotions and instinctively know what will cause people pain and discomfort. But they are lacking in affective empathy, which allows them to internalize and experience what another person is feeling. Affective empathy is also what leads people to be kind and compassionate toward another person. It keeps people from saying or doing mean things. But trolls understand what will hurt people and then act on it without concern for how it will make them feel.

Motivating Factors

While a troll or a flamer's personality plays a large role in why they do what they do, they also might be motivated by other factors. Here is a closer look at

Sometimes trolls think they are hilarious when they post hurtful jokes online. They crave the attention and don't care that their jabs are far from funny for the victim.

some of the things that might motivate someone to troll or flame another person.

- *Gain attention.* Sometimes trolls are looking to get attention, even if it is negative attention. Heated debates can make them feel important, perhaps more than they do in real life. And even if people ignore them, they rarely suffer any type of public humiliation. They are usually anonymous. No one really knows who they are. They can seek attention without risk of being embarrassed.

- *Be funny.* There are trolls who think that what they are saying online is funny and they are hoping just to get a laugh. Unfortunately, jokes do not always go over very well online and many jokes fall flat or are misinterpreted. As a result, trolling behavior is rarely funny. Yet, trolls and flamers will continue to make jokes at other people's expenses.

- *Alleviate boredom.* When trolls or flamers are bored, they turn to trolling and flaming as a way to add some excitement and drama to their lives. Creating digital drama keeps them entertained and they enjoy making others uncomfortable. Many times, trolls have very few friends and not much of a social life. They spend their free time online wreaking havoc in other people's lives.

- *Seek revenge.* Sometimes people troll or flame others because they are angry or upset. As a result, they troll the person's page hoping to cause them pain and discomfort. They justify their behavior by telling themselves that the victim deserves it.

Hunting for Trolls

Ever wondered if there was a way to spot trolls before they do too much damage? Researchers from Stanford and Cornell Universities may have found a way. They developed an algorithm that predicts if someone is a potential troll. An algorithm is a set of instructions or guidelines that tell a computer what to do. The algorithm they created needs to see only five to ten online posts before it predicts whether or not a commenter is a troll.

Before developing the algorithm, the researchers studied internet trolls over time to see what caused them to be banned from discussion groups. The study, which was funded by Google, found that trolls usually have poor spelling and grammar and they tend to post a lot. Their posts also are usually of poor quality and harder to understand. And the posts usually include negative words and profanity.

The researchers feel that algorithms like this may be useful to online moderators because it would help them identify trolls much earlier. But it is not foolproof. In fact, one in five people that the algorithm identified as a future troll never turned out to cause trouble online. As a result, identifying trolls still will require some human effort.

Ten Trolls and Flamers You Might Encounter Online

No one troll is exactly like another. Trolls do not fit neatly into one category. In fact, they can vary greatly. They have different personalities, goals, and behaviors. What's more, some trolls will fall into several categories and some will be in a category all their own. Here is an overview of the ten most common types of trolls you might encounter online.

Haters

Just like the name implies, this type of troll is hateful toward other people. And they don't even have to have a reason to hate or insult others. They simply look for opportunities and then exploit them. For instance, a hater might dis your favorite sports team, the band you mention, or even your school. Or they might call you names or make accusations.

Haters will do whatever they can to get a negative emotional response from you just because they can. Sometimes, haters go beyond trolling and engage in hate speech. When this happens their attacks involve racism, sexism, homophobia, and religious intolerance.

Debate Mongers

This type of troll loves a good argument. They are convinced they are right and that everyone else is wrong. Even when the facts clearly show that their views are invalid, they will take the opposing side. Typically, this type of troll will leave long comments or arguments that are often tiresome to read. And, they will keep posting until other commenters give up. They are intent on having the last word.

Another version of the debate monger is more of a show-off. This type of troll loves to share his or her opinion in extreme detail. These trolls are the online version of the person who loves to hear his own voice. They will write really long comments or posts with little concern for whether anyone reads them. Their motivation is simply showing the world how much they think they know about a given subject.

Hijackers

This type of troll will comment on another person's post but with something that is off topic. For instance, the post could be about dealing with cats when someone starts commenting about their dog. If the person posting about their dog wanted to discuss their dog, they should have started their own discussion.

Instead, they hijack the original poster's audience to talk about something completely different. And if successful, everyone ends up talking about what the hijacker posted and forgets about the original post. This type of trolling happens all the time, especially on Facebook, Twitter, and in YouTube comments.

White Knights

These trolls see themselves as heroes and are the first to jump into a discussion if they think someone has hurt another person's feelings. But instead of doing good, they end up causing a lot of harm because they aggravate the situation by throwing out insults and profanity-laced comments in defense of the victim. What usually happens is that the original discussion is forgotten and the victim is trapped in a flame war between the white knight and the other commenters.

Pretenders

Pretenders are liars and the most common type of troll on the internet. These trolls pretend to be someone they are not. For instance, mean girls engage in catfishing and try to lure other girls into a fake relationship. Meanwhile, an online predator stalks young women by pretending to be a boy their age. Either way, these trolls are posers pretending to be someone they are not.

They lie about everything—who they are, what they do, and even what they look like. And when their fake identity stops working for them, they will simply disappear and reinvent themselves. Eventually, they will show up again with a new name, a new picture, and a new identity.

Trolls enjoy creating trouble online. They cannot wait for others to make mistakes so they can pull out their virtual flamethrowers and torch everyone in their paths.

Fire Starters

These trolls like to make trouble just for the pure enjoyment of it. Many times, they don't wait for someone to slip up online. Instead, they pull out their virtual flamethrower and torch everyone in their path with mean words, name-calling, and accusations. What's more, this troll rarely backs down even if others show him where he is wrong. It is best not to engage with this troll at all and instead block him because he destroys everyone and everything in his path with his flaming.

Mean Girls (and Guys)

You know this troll. She is the mean girl who rules your school with nasty words and exclusive cliques, and if she decides to troll you online, it can get really ugly. Not only will she troll everything from what you wear to what you say, but she also will go back in time to every post you have ever made to find something embarrassing to exploit.

For this troll, it is all about power and popularity. She craves both and will stop at nothing to get it. And if she thinks trolling you will help her get there, watch out. This troll will exploit and expose anything she can get her hands on. If you find yourself in her crosshairs, unfortunately you need to be careful what you post. She will use anything she can in an effort to discredit you and make you look bad.

Spammers

Spammers are selfish trolls who do not care about your post or discussion. Instead, they are using your audience to benefit themselves. He wants you to check out his page, follow the link he posted, buy his book, or follow him. These trolls are annoying but rarely do much damage unless their links contain a virus or a scam.

Meme Junkies

This type of troll lacks creativity and will often rely on memes to disrupt posts or wreak havoc. Instead

Instead of preparing a thoughtful comment, some trolls and flamers disrupt posts with memes—such as Grumpy Cat, shown here—until people leave the discussion or block them.

51

of making a comment, this troll will just post a meme. And he will often continue to post memes until people get really angry, leave the discussion, or block him.

Grammar Nazis

This type of troll might embarrass you, and can be really annoying, but other than that they are typically harmless. The grammar nazi is obsessed with proper spelling and grammar. As a result, they are the ones who feel compelled to tell others that they have misspelled words and made punctuation errors.

In extreme cases, some of them will use a commenter's spelling and grammar mistakes as an excuse to insult them. No matter what topic is being discussed, these types of trolls zero in on the one word you used incorrectly like "there" instead of "their" or "they're."

Self-Trolling: Why Kids Harm Themselves Online

Psychiatrists are just beginning to study the new phenomenon of self-trolling, in which kids post hateful and mean comments about themselves online. But instead of just sharing

Self-trolling occurs when kids post hateful or mean comments about themselves online. Instead of sharing their self-hatred openly, they pretend to be a troll, flamer, or cyberbully.

their self-hatred openly, they disguise themselves as trolls, flamers, and cyberbullies. In the end, their friends, teachers, and parents think they are being attacked online but in reality, they are doing all the trolling and flaming themselves.

According to some researchers, self-trolling is probably more common than we might imagine. In fact, the Massachusetts Aggression Reduction Center found that about 15 percent of eighteen-year-olds posted a cruel remark about themselves.

But the number of kids engaging in self-trolling may be even higher. Experts say that getting young people to disclose their self-trolling is extremely difficult because of the shame associated with the behavior. Of the kids who do self-troll, approximately 60 percent repeat the behavior. What's more, self-trollers also report more depression and anxiety and are less popular in school.

Researchers who study self-trolling believe that it is way for teens to release self-hatred and anxiety. It also becomes a way to gain attention while seeing how others respond. For instance, will their peers agree with the comments made or provide comfort instead? What they are seeking is not only attention, but also compliments and encouragement to drown the negative self-talk they have in their heads.

Self-trolling also can be a tool to try to look like someone who is popular enough to attract a bunch of "haters." Yet, many who have self-trolled said that leaving nasty comments about themselves made them feel worse and did not get them more attention.

Finally, researchers stress that digital self-harm is not the only explanation for the negative, anonymous comments left online. In fact, actual trolls do the majority of trolling and flaming. But the fact that self-trolling exists should not be overlooked.

The next time someone is trolled, find out how they are doing and if they need a little more support. Regardless of whether the troll is a stranger or the victim disguised as someone else, the victim of trolling still needs your encouragement.

CHAPTER FOUR

Are You at Risk?

Kathy Sierra, a computer programming instructor, game developer, and author, believes that you are most at risk for trolling when you are getting a lot of visibility online. In other words, people are listening, following, liking, favoriting, and retweeting what you have to say.

"From the hater's [point of view] you do not deserve that attention," says Sierra, who was trolled so badly at one point that she was afraid to leave the house. "[To trolls] you are stealing an audience. [And], the idea that others listen to you is insanity . . . That just can't be allowed."

Trolls get it in their heads that you must be stopped, she explains. "And if they cannot stop you, they can at least ruin your quality of life. A standard goal in troll culture . . . is to cause personal ruin." Some trolls are sociopaths that are "doing it out of pure malice, for 'lulz'" and they are masters at manipulating public perception, she says.

The trolling Sierra experienced was so significant that she nearly left the technology industry. She also deleted her online presence. But in 2013, she started venturing back into the online world again with a blog called *Serious Pony*. She also wrote a book in 2015, *Badass: Making Users Awesome*. To date, she still doesn't have a Twitter account because of how many trolls use it to hurt people.

Who Let the Trolls Out? Bad Habits That Attract Trolls and Flamers

Like Kathy Sierra, you should *never* blame yourself for being trolled or flamed online. For instance, your success in school or sports may attract the attention of trolls, but you do not deserve to be trolled. Or, you may be really good at photography and have a large following on Instagram, but that does not mean you should be trolled. These things may attract the attention of trolls and sometimes there is not much you can do stop the hate, but you are never to blame. You also should not stop living your life to its fullest.

But there are things that you may unknowingly do that make you more susceptible to trolling, such as oversharing or posting too many selfies. These are the things that you need to address in order to help prevent trolling in your life. The following are some common ways kids (and sometimes adults) attract the attention of trolls.

Oversharing Information

The concept of oversharing is especially important online. For instance, if you share every detail about your life online, you are opening yourself up to trolling and gossip. What's more, this information gives trolls ammunition that they can use against you. Not only can they blow these details out of proportion, but they also can take the things you posted out of context. This information is then twisted into something completely different. A good rule of thumb is to keep your posts general. Do not post about the fight you had with your parents, the drama that exists on your soccer team, or the spat you had with your friend. Settle those things offline.

Taking Too Many Selfies

Everyone loves to post selfies, especially if you are doing something fun like attending a concert or spending time in a gorgeous location, such as at the beach. But there are two problems with selfies. First, they are pictures of you that can be downloaded and used in a troll's blogs, posts, and tweets. Second, they

Posting too many selfies can put you at risk for trolling and flaming. Trolls may view your selfies and assume your life is perfect. Their goal becomes making your life miserable.

also can attract the attention of trolls and flamers, especially if they struggle with envy and jealousy. A troll could view your selfie and assume your life is perfect. Their goal then becomes making your life miserable. While you can still post selfies from time to time, it is important that you do so in moderation.

Engaging in Subtweeting and Vaguebooking

Contrary to what you think, posting vague tweets and posts online, known as subtweeting and vaguebooking, is never subtle. Usually people know exactly whom you are talking about. And even if they do not, they can use these passive-aggressive posts to troll you. To stay under a troll's radar, keep your posts and tweets upbeat and refrain from vaguebooking and subtweeting.

Participating in Sexting

Aside from the fact that sexting is wrong and has a number of legal and emotional consequences, it also can lead to trolling and flaming online. Anytime you send a sext to another person, you lose control over the image. As a result, it is very easy for your images to end up online. And when they do, the trolling will be relentless. Not only can sexting ruin your reputation, but recovering from the shaming that occurs afterwards is extremely difficult. Countless young people have taken their lives because private sext messages were shared online. Consequently, they were trolled so relentlessly that they felt the pain and humiliation would never end.

Taking Part in Heated Discussions

It is very important to control your anger, especially online. Sure, people find it entertaining to watch you lose your temper or to take down others with your knowledge about a particular subject, but doing so sets you up for trolling. Heated discussions and debates are better handled in person. Even then, it's best to remain calm. It is all too easy for people to videotape you and later post it online. Likewise, trolls may use screenshots from the video to develop memes and harass you further.

Exaggerating the Truth Online

Never make up things to appear differently online. The truth is almost always revealed. What's more, if you are dishonest online and then later targeted by trolls, people will readily believe the lies others say about you, even if you deny them. Remember, trolls use a lot of embellishment to make their claims believable. But if you have a track record for being honest and truthful, it will be much easier to set the record straight.

Flirting with Someone's Significant Other

Nothing puts you at greater risk for flaming, trolling, and even cyberbullying than making advances toward another person's boyfriend or girlfriend. It is just common courtesy to respect the natural boundaries of relationships. If you do not respect those boundaries, then you are surely setting yourself up for trolling not only from the injured party but from everyone else who will come to her defense. Remember, no matter how much you like someone, it is not worth getting trolled over.

Steps You Can Take to Prevent Trolling and Flaming

While you cannot completely protect yourself from trolling, there are some things that you can do that will help you stay protected online and under the radar. Here are some other suggestions that will help keep you safe online.

Conduct a Social Media Audit

Go through your social media accounts once a month and look at what you are posting and retweeting. Do the things in your feed still represent who you are

Flirting with someone else's boyfriend puts you at risk for trolling. Show common courtesy and respect the natural boundary of relationships. It is not worth getting trolled over.

and what you want to say to the world? If not, then delete them from your feed. It is also a good idea to be careful about what posts, tweets, and comments you like or favorite. Even though you are not the original poster, the fact that you like or favorite the content sends a message about you as a person.

The Three Cs of Online Behavior

According to Sue Scheff, an internet safety advocate and author of *Shame Nation*, "One way kids can curb online trolling is by limiting their sharing and being mindful with their posts. Oversharing is probably one of the most common ways people get themselves in trouble online."

As a result, she recommends that teens follow the three Cs of online behavior.

1. *Conduct.* Control yourself, she says. Remember there is another person on the other side of the screen.

2. *Content.* Limit your sharing. Will it embarrass or humiliate you or someone else?

3. *Caring.* Make sure everything you post online is done with empathy and kindness.

Turn Off Geotagging

Trolls love to share personal information such as home addresses, school locations, and even your favorite coffee house. As a result, remember your photos can give away your locations. Aside from the camera on your smartphone, a number of social media platforms use geotagging as well, including Instagram and Facebook. So, be sure this function is turned off before posting online. You also may want to refrain from posting about an event you are attending or a vacation you are on until after you are home. This way, trolls and other predators cannot track you down in real time.

Practice Good Digital Etiquette

Never forget the importance of being respectful and kind online. Basically, the same rules of courtesy and empathy apply online as they do in person. Remember, it is way too easy to say things from behind a keyboard than it is to say them in person. As a result, stop and think before you post. Would you still make the same comment if the person were standing right in front of you? What would people you respect—your mom, your teacher, your coach, or your pastor—think of this post? Sometimes asking yourself those simple questions will keep you from posting something you might later regret or that a troll or flamer could use to burn you.

Choose Strong Privacy Settings

Go through all your social media accounts, your email, and even your computer and make sure that you are using the best privacy settings you can. For instance, you should consider changing the privacy settings on Instagram from the default setting of public to private. Doing so ensures that you have a little more control over your photos. This way, the people you allow to follow you are the only ones who can view them. Keep in mind this protection is not foolproof. People can still copy and share your images, but at least you can control who has access to them originally.

Block and Report Questionable Social Media Posts

If you see someone online who shares inappropriate photos, makes rude comments, or trolls others, consider blocking him and reporting his behavior to the social media platform. Although it may take some time for the provider to respond to your complaint, you will have in the meantime protected yourself from becoming a victim of trolling.

Stay Away from Mean Girls, Bullies, and Cliques

Although this is obvious advice, many young people want to climb the social ladder at school, so they develop friendships with questionable people. But these types of people often use weapons like trolling, flaming, and cyberbullying to wield social power. And there is no guarantee that they won't target you, too.

Select Strong Passwords

It is not uncommon for trolls to impersonate people online. As a result, you need to do everything you can to prevent someone from hacking into your account. For this reason, you should choose passwords that will be easy for you to remember, but very difficult for someone else to figure out. One option might

Trolls often impersonate other people. To avoid becoming a victim, do everything you can to prevent people from hacking into your account, including picking a strong password.

If you are trolled online, remember this simple rule: honesty is the best policy. Acknowledge the facts and leave it at that.

be selecting a word, or better yet, a short phrase that means something to you and replacing some of the letters with numbers or symbols. For example, you can replace the letter "I" with the number one or an exclamation point and the letter "E" with the number three.

Remember Honesty Is Always the Best Policy

Lastly, if you do become a victim of trolling, do not play dumb or pretend that you have no idea what people are saying about you online. Acting clueless or not acknowledging what is happening sometimes makes people you know believe that what others are saying is true. Instead, when people ask about the trolling, you could respond: "I know what people are saying online. But what they are saying is not true."

Then, calmly tell them what is true and leave it at that. Try not to raise your voice or get emotional when you are clearing the air. The goal is to remain in control of your emotions while being as authentic as you can. Focus on setting the record straight and then move on. You should never dwell on what the troll has said or done because then others will dwell on it as well.

CHAPTER FIVE

What You Can Do if You Are a Victim

According to Sue Scheff, internet safety advocate and author of *Shame Nation*, it takes a long time to get over a trolling incident. "This is not something you just move forward from easily," she explains. "First you have to accept that it happened. You have to be angry about it and you have to take care of yourself. It took me a long time to say 'I matter.'"

Scheff was trolled by a disgruntled woman who was on a mission to destroy her and her organization, she says. "As with many trolling situations, her online smear campaign attracted many others—that didn't even know me—but just figured it was fun to throw mud," she explains. "It truly defines the gang-like mentality of how trolls act online."

The woman's trolling left Scheff emotionally and financially crippled, she says. Eventually, she took legal action against the woman for internet defamation and invasion of privacy and won a $11.3 million landmark case. She goes into detail about the trolling and her lawsuit in her book, *Google Bomb*. But, even though her name was cleared, Scheff says what is troubling is that "Google never says I am sorry."

When people take a part of your life and completely turn it around, it can be devastating, she adds. "It wasn't only the lies, it was the twisted truths that really were horrifying. There is absolutely nothing worse [than being trolled]. I went to a completely dark place in my life."

"I had to close my office, not only for financial reasons, but emotionally," she says. "I was broken. I rarely left the house and never gave out my name for fear people would Google me. Every day I woke up, I feared what the internet had to say about me. When people would tell me, I would cringe."

Today, Scheff makes peace with what happened to her by helping other people. "My way of healing is being an activist and sharing ways for people to work on their online presence. I teach people how to prevent online shaming and how to survive trolling."

Taking Yourself Out of Harm's Way

It can feel devastating to experience trolling and flaming online. But your life will get better, Scheff insists. It's also important to remember that there are people who will help you and support you.

Experiencing trolling and flaming online feels devastating. But remember, your life will get better. There are people who will help you and support you. Just reach out.

She says,

"Never think that you have to deal with trolling alone. Tell a friend or an adult. So many kids keep this festered up inside of them. There are so many people out there that care about them. Thinking you're alone and people *are laughing at you is horrible. You have to know that is not accurate."*

When you first go through trolling, it can be hard to know what to do. But experts like Scheff suggest that you start with the basics like reporting and blocking the troll. Here is a list of the first things you should do when you are confronted by a troll.

- *Refrain from responding.* Sometimes the best way to deal with a troll is to ignore posts, comments, texts, and calls. Although it can be tempting to respond or to correct the troll, this is rarely successful. In fact, trolls often use your comments and reactions against you. The best advice is to avoid giving them more material to work with. Remember, most of the time responding to a troll causes the situation to escalate.

- *Block and report the troll.* One of the first things you should do is block the troll from your social media platform. You also should screenshot the comments and report the troll to the community forum, social media platform, or any other service where the troll keeps popping up. Sites like Instagram, Facebook, and Twitter will investigate claims of trolling. Even if the trolling is anonymous or occurs under a fake account, you should report it.

- *Contact the police immediately regarding any threats.* Remember that threats of rape, death, beating, strangulation, and other physical violence are against the law and should be reported. Stalking behavior along with harassment based on gender, race, religion, or disability should also be reported. Even suggestions to commit suicide should be reported to police. They will address these situations.

- *Cut off access.* Make it hard for trolls to find you. Cancel your current social networking accounts like Instagram, Facebook, and Twitter. (You can open new accounts if you want.) No longer allow comments on your YouTube channel and blogs. You can also control your privacy on Facebook, and even who can post on your page. Change your email address. Get an unlisted cell phone number, then block the troll from your phone. The goal is to make it very difficult for the troll to find you.

- *Become a self-advocate.* If there is something you need that will help you deal with trolling, speak up and ask for it. Self-advocacy skills are some of the most important skills you will need in life not only for dealing with trolls but also for dealing with whatever comes your way. They also are an important part of the

Remember to ask for help if you are trolled. Becoming a self-advocate is one of the most important skills you need. Self-advocacy helps you take control of your life.

healing process. These skills will help you not only become confident again, but empower you to take control over your life again.

Things to Remember as You Move Forward After Trolling

Once you have addressed the basics of getting the trolling to stop, it can still be hard to deal with the aftermath. Trolling often leaves you feeling alone, confused, embarrassed, and isolated. But if you focus on making healthy choices and taking care of yourself, in time, you will feel better. Here are some things all victims of trolling should remember as they heal from trolling.

Avoid People Who Thrive on Drama

If your goal is to remain positive about your situation, you cannot afford to be around people who live for drama, gossip, and rumors. What's more, you should avoid people who simply want to hear what is going on with your situation. These people are looking for a juicy story. People who care about you ask what they can do to help you. If you want to talk, they will listen. And if you want to cry, they will lend you their shoulder. At this point in your life, it is a good idea to tighten your circle of friends to those you can trust and who are committed to supporting you.

Remember: It's Not the End of the World if Some People Don't Like You

Never waste your time and energy trying to please everyone or trying to get people to like you. Instead, focus on being a good friend, having integrity, and remaining true to who you are. If you focus on being a good person rather than trying to win the approval of

Supportive friends are important to moving on. Do not waste your time with people who live for gossip and rumors. Tighten your circle of friends to those who are trustworthy.

77

other people, your friendships will happen naturally. Never compromise who you are just so you can fit in. This can be particularly tempting after you have been trolled. It is not uncommon to believe there is something wrong with you. But do not give in to this notion. Instead, embrace who you are.

Let Go of the Desire for Revenge

While it is often a natural reaction to want revenge for being trolled, it will never make you feel better. Instead, focus on forgiveness. But be patient with yourself. Forgiveness is a decision that will take time. What's more, forgiveness is not about excusing the troll's actions; it's about releasing the hold the trolling and flaming has over your life. Forgiveness takes away the power trolls have over you. What's more, you are able to stop dwelling on what the trolls did and move on. They are still wrong and responsible for what they did, but their actions no longer have a hold on you.

Be Aware of the Effects of Trolling

When you have been trolled online, it is normal to experience a wide variety of emotions and physical responses. For instance, you may feel everything from overwhelmed and vulnerable to depressed and anxious. And while these are normal responses, they are not feelings you should learn to live with. As a result, do not be afraid to ask for help in coping with

It is normal to experience a variety of emotions to trolling and flaming, but do not assume you have to live with these negative feelings. Ask for help.

trolling. Trolling is not something you should go through alone. It's best to build a support network to help you work through all that you are feeling.

Consider Counseling

Trolling is a big issue that shouldn't be handled alone. At the very least, you should surround yourself with supportive friends and family. It is essential that you have one or two people with whom you can talk about what is happening. You also should consider talking with a counselor in order to heal, especially if you are experiencing changes in mood, sleeping habits, or eating habits.

Remember You Are Never Truly Alone

It is normal to feel alone, hopeless, and vulnerable when you experience trolling and flaming. But it is important to remember that you are never truly alone. There is always someone out there who cares about you and supports you. Too many times, teens start to believe the lies that trolls post and end up considering drastic measures to cope with their situations.

Scheff says she can see how teens would be tempted to do something drastic. "I know that deep, dark hole that I was in and realize that at one point, death could have been the easy way out," she says. "I completely understand the Tyler Clementi,

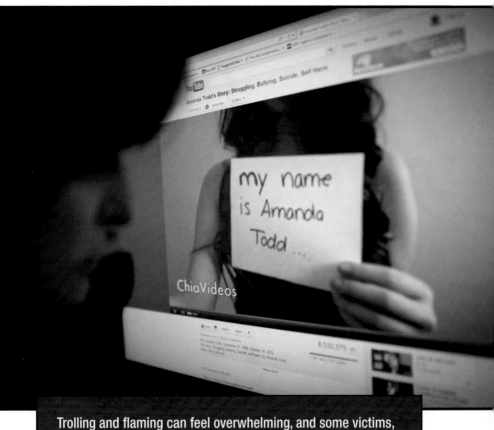

Trolling and flaming can feel overwhelming, and some victims, like Amanda Todd, feel like there is no escape. But remember, this experience will not go on forever.

Amanda Todd and Rebecca Sedwicks out there who were humiliated to death. I get it. I was lucky. I was mature enough to know that this shall pass. Kids don't always know that. That is why I am so passionate about this topic."

Trolling is not worth losing a life over. Never give a troll that much power. You have value and worth.

10 Great Questions to Ask a Counselor

If you are struggling with trolling in your life, you may have questions like those listed here. If you are struggling with any of these issues, find a trusted adult, such as a parent, teacher, or counselor to discuss your questions with.

1. How can I tell if I am being trolled online?

2. Where can I go to get help?

3. How can I get the trolling to stop?

4. Is there a way to get people to accept me?

5. Why does trolling hurt so much?

6. Why do people judge others online?

7. Is there a way to stay safe online without giving up social media?

8. What do you think I should do about trolling?

9. I am having trouble ignoring the trolling; what do you suggest?

10. What can I do to feel better about myself?

CHAPTER SIX

What Can You Do About Flaming and Trolling?

When Olivia was being trolled in seventh grade, she says one of the hardest parts to deal with was the fact that so many people would scroll past the Instagram posts where she was being victimized and not do anything about it. No one reached out to her. No one asked how she was doing. Rarely did someone post positive comments to outweigh the mean ones.

She says it hurt that no one seemed to defend her or stand up for her. "It was, in all honesty, like I was in my own bubble," she says. "People kept passing by me and letting it happen. I kept thinking I would get over it. But I didn't. And, I started to

Remember that a simple positive post can outweigh the cruel and hurtful comments and remind the victim that she is not alone.

struggle with depression and anxiety. I also felt scared and timid most of the time."

Although Olivia's experience is not uncommon, it does not have to be that way. Bystanders to online cruelty have more power than they might realize. In fact, a simple kind statement can change another person's impression of the situation.

Zipped Lips: Why Bystanders Often Do Nothing About Trolling

Most people know that trolling is wrong and hurtful. Yet, they just cannot bring themselves to intervene even though witnessing trolling and flaming online can be a troubling experience. In fact, many kids who see trolling online often feel anxious and helpless. But, very few kids will do anything about it. Not only do they fail to stand up for the victim, they also never report what they see. Here are the top reasons why mum's the word when trolling happens online:

- *Fear the troll will retaliate.* Fear is perhaps the top reason that people stay silent when they see trolling or flaming. They are afraid of becoming a target as well. This belief is especially true for bystanders that have been victimized by trolls in the past. They see trolling and are simply glad it is someone else and not them.

- *Believe it is none of their business.* Most of the time, people try to stay out of situations that do not involve them. While that is a good practice when it comes to normal conflict involving other people, it is not good advice when online trolling occurs. When trolling occurs, victims need to know that they are not alone. They need to feel supported.
- *Feel the victim deserves it.* Sometimes people make judgments about victims of trolling. For example, the bystander might feel like the target of trolling was "annoying" or "shared too much information" and that he or she deserve to be flamed. But everyone deserves to be treated with respect. And trolls are not respectful.

Until these belief systems are changed, teens will continue to zip their lips when they see trolling unfold online. Instead, they need to view trolling as unacceptable online behavior and be willing to stand up for victims when they see it occur.

Tips for Putting a Lid on Trolling

Although bystanders are neither trolls nor victims, they are still affected by the negative online environment that trolling creates. Some studies even

Victims of trolling and flaming need to know that they are not alone. Feeling supported and valued helps eliminate feelings of helplessness.

suggest that bystanders may suffer just as much as the victim. As a result, it is important the bystanders know how to address trolling even when it is affecting someone else. Here are some things that anyone can do to help a victim of trolling and help put an end to flaming and trolling once and for all.

- *Support the victim.* Sometimes the best way to help is to offer an encouraging word to the victim. Remind her that she does not deserve this treatment, that it is unfair, and that it is untrue. Deep down, most victims realize that trolling is wrong. But if no one else makes a point to say it as well, it can be tempting to believe the words the troll is saying.
- *Offer to help.* In other words, encourage the victim of trolling to take healthy steps toward ending the trolling behavior. For example, discourage her from responding aggressively or trying to get revenge. Instead encourage her to report the trolling and block the troll from communicating with her further.
- *Show a trusted adult.* If you witness trolling online, talk to a trusted adult about what you are witnessing. For example, if there are threats of violence or other crimes, the police should be contacted. This is much easier to accomplish with an adult helping you relay the information.
- *Consider taking a stand.* If you feel safe doing so, take a stand by commenting on the post, photo, or in the comment section. Make sure your

You can help a victim of trolling by encouraging and supporting her. Remind her that she is valuable and worthwhile and should never seek revenge.

words are neutral and not laced with anything negative or rude. For instance, you could say something like: "I am removing myself from this thread because it is mean and hurtful."

89

Don't Make a Bad Situation Worse

Sometimes people make trolling worse without even realizing it. Here are some things to avoid when you see trolling online:

Liking or commenting on posts, images, and videos that are hurtful to other people. Remember, when it comes to trolling, there is no such thing as harmless fun.

Forwarding or sharing screenshots of trolling or flaming online. Your goal should always be to put an end to the hate, not spread it.

Laughing or joining in on the trolling. Even though you may not have started the trolling behavior, if you join in you are just as guilty as the troll. Resist the urge to gang up on another person.

Scrolling past mean comments and posts without doing anything. Offer support to the victim by posting something positive or sending her a private message. Your silence could be misinterpreted as agreement with what is being said.

Telling yourself it's none of your business. Staying neutral never makes trolling end, and it never helps someone fight the despair that bullying causes. Your kind words could have a bigger impact than you ever realized.

- *Ask others to join you.* Sometimes it is safer, and more effective, if a group of people takes away a troll or flamer's audience. Remember, there is strength in numbers. So if you take a stand encourage others to follow your lead and leave the thread. Even if they don't, you are doing the right thing and have taken away some of the troll's power.

- *Check back in with the victim.* Sometimes sending just one positive note is not enough to get a person through a trolling incident. Show the victim that not all people are rude by sending another message of encouragement. Remind her that she did not deserve to be trolled online and that none of the things the troll said about her are true.

Change Starts with You

While it can be hard to take that first step toward standing up for a victim, it needs to be done. If you want social media to be a kinder, happier place where people post positive pictures and comments, then you need to realize that you can play a part in that.

Too many times, people worry about what victims should do when they are confronting trolls, such as not responding directly, blocking the troll,

Sending a positive text or posting a kind word can remind a trolling victim that not all people are cruel, heartless, and mean.

and reporting his behavior. But what if bystanders like you raised their voices as well?

The first step may be to simply take away the attention that trolls desperately crave. Instead of telling the troll he is wrong, rude, or mean, focus all your energy on the victim. Say something nice. Offer a compliment. Encourage her to keep being who she is. Send her a private message letting her know that what she is experiencing is wrong and that it is not her

End trolling by taking away the attention that the flamer desperately craves. Instead, focus on the victim by saying something nice or offering a compliment.

fault. Encourage others to leave the thread and ignore the troll. Whatever it is you do, support the victim as best as you can, and take away the troll's audience.

You may be powerless to change the trolls, but you are not powerless when it comes to supporting victims and making online communities a more positive space. The key is to realize that change starts with you.

Stop scrolling past the mean posts and comments in silence. Pause and say something nice. This small step may be exactly what the victim of trolling needs to hear. And it may be just what is needed to send trolls scrambling back into the shadows.

Glossary

affective empathy The ability to internalize and experience what another person is feeling; it leads people to be kind and compassionate toward another person.

algorithm A set of instructions or guidelines that tell a computer what to do.

atypical Not normal, regular, or usual.

cognitive empathy The ability to understand people's emotions and instinctively know what causes people pain and discomfort.

catfishing Trying to lure another person into a fake relationship.

character assassination A malicious, harmful, and untrue attempt to damage someone's reputation.

cyberbullying Bullying that takes place over digital devices like laptops, tablets, and smartphones; it includes sending, posting, and sharing negative, harmful, false, or mean content about someone else in an attempt to ruin their reputation.

flames Insults that are traded back and forth online that usually are rude and include profanity.

flaming A hostile and insulting interaction between people online that usually involves profanity.

geotagging The process of adding location and other geographical information to photos and other media on digital devices.

integrity Having the characteristic of being honest and sincere.

lulz A slang term referring to having fun or laughing at another person's expense.

oversharing Sharing too much personal information online.

psychopaths People who do not feel empathy, guilt, remorse, or responsibility for their actions.

public perception A virtual truth shaped by the media, online posts, trolling, and other activities.

sadistic When people enjoy causing other people physical and psychological pain.

screenshot A photo of what is displayed on a digital device such as a smartphone or a tablet; sometimes called a screen capture.

sexting Nude and sexually explicit photographs or messages shared via mobile phone.

social media audit The process of going through all your social media accounts to make sure all the posts, tweets, and photos still represent the message you want the rest of the world to hear.

social rewards A term psychologists use to refer to rewards that involve acceptance, popularity, and likability.

subtweeting Posting a vague tweet on Twitter about someone without identifying who you are talking about.

trolling When a person attacks another person online for their thoughts, beliefs, opinions, or physical appearance.

trolls People who intentionally aggravate others online by posting offensive comments, content, or pictures.

vaguebooking Posting a vague post or comment on Facebook about someone without identifying the person you are talking about.

For More Information

ConnectSafely
Website: http://www.connectsafely.org/about-us
Facebook and Twitter: @connectsafely
Contact via the online form: http://www
.connectsafely.org/about-us/contact
Connect Safely is a nonprofit organization dedicated to educating people about safety, privacy, and security both while using technology and while on the internet. They offer safety tips, guidebooks, advice, and news about the technology industry.

Crisis Text Line
Email: support@crisistextline.org
Website: https://www.crisistextline.org
Facebook and Instagram: @crisistextline
Twitter: @CrisisTextLine
Crisis Text Line is a free, 24/7 text messaging service that offers support for young people in crisis. Teens who want to communicate with a trained crisis counselor text 741741 from anywhere in the United States.

Cyber Civil Rights Initiative
University of Miami School of Law
1311 Miller Road, G-378
Coral Gables, FL 33146
(850) 410-3800

Website: https://www.cybercivilrights.org
Facebook: @CyberCivilRightsInitiative
Twitter: @CCRInitiative
The purpose of the Cyber Civil Rights Initiative
is to fight nonconsensual pornography
(sometimes called revenge porn) and other
forms of online abuse. The organization
provides referral services, collaborates
with the tech industry, and advocates for
legislation. It also offers a twenty-four-hour
crisis helpline.

Get Cyber Safe (Canada)
(613) 944-4875 or (800) 830-3118
Email: info@Getcybersafe.gc.ca
Website: https://www.getcybersafe.gc.ca
Facebook: @GetCyberSafe
Twitter and Instagram: @getcybersafe
Get Cyber Safe is an online resource designed
to educate Canadians about how to stay safe
online. They offer information for adults,
teens, and businesses.

National Crime Prevention Council
1201 Connecticut Avenue, NW, Suite 200
Washington DC 20036
(202) 466-6272
Website: http://www.ncpc.org

Facebook: @McGruff

Twitter: @McGruffatNCPC

The National Crime Prevention Council is dedicated to helping people keep themselves, their families, and their communities safe from crime. The organization is most recognizable for McGruff the Crime Dog, who "takes a bite out of crime."

Online SOS Network

Email: support@onlinesos.zendesk.com

Website: https://www.onlinesosnetwork.org

Facebook: @onlinesosnetwork

Twitter: @onlinesosorg

Online SOS provides confidential, professional support to people experiencing online harassment. They are trained to deal with trolling, cyberbullying, stalking, threats of violence, distribution of private information, impersonation, hacking, nonconsensual pornography, and other forms of harassment.

Pew Research Center

1615 L Street, NW, Suite 700

Washington, DC 20036

(202) 419-4300

Website: www.pewresearch.org

Facebook and Twitter: @pewresearch

The Pew Research Center is a fact tank created to inform the public about issues, attitudes, and trends that shape the country. They conduct public opinion polling, demographic research, and other social science research.

Tyler Clementi Foundation

104 West 29th Street, 11th Floor

New York, NY 10001

(646) 871-8095

Website: https://tylerclementi.org

Facebook: @TheTylerClementiFoundation

Twitter: @TylerClementi

Instagram: @tyler_clementi_foundation

The Tyler Clementi Foundation was created by the Clementi family to honor the memory of Tyler Clementi. Their goal is to prevent online and offline bullying through inclusion, assertion of dignity, and acceptance.

For Further Reading

Adams, Sabrina. *Everything You Need to Know About Trolls and Cybermobs*. New York, NY: Rosen Publishing, 2017.

Cunningham, Anne. *Public Shaming* (Opposing Viewpoints). New York, NY: Greenhaven Publishing, 2017.

Gordon, Sherri Mabry. *Are You at Risk for Public Shaming?* (Got Issues?). New York, NY: Enslow Publishing, 2016.

Leavitt, Aimee Jane. *Combatting Toxic Online Communities*. New York, NY: Rosen Publishing, 2016.

McAneney, Caitlin. *I Have Been Cyberbullied. Now What?* New York, NY: Rosen Publishing, 2015.

McKee, Jonathan. *The Teen's Guide to Social Media . . . and Mobile Devices: 21 Tips to Wise Posting in an Insecure World*. Uhrichsville, OH: Shiloh Run Press, 2017.

Morin, Amy. *13 Things Mentally Strong People Don't Do*. New York, NY: William Morrow, 2014.

Orr, Tamra B. *I Have Been Shamed on the Internet. Now What?* New York, NY: Rosen Publishing, 2017.

Patchin, Justin W., and Hinduja, Sameer. *Words Wound: Delete Cyberbullying and Make Kindness Go Viral*. Minneapolis, MN: Free Spirit Publishing, 2013.

Bibliography

Buoni, Olivia. Interview with author, October 2017.

Carey, Tanith. "The Teens Who Troll Themselves." *Daily Mail*, February 26, 2014. http://www.dailymail.co.uk/femail/article-2568762/The-teens-troll-In-shocking-new-form-self-harming-young-people-vile-online-bullies.html.

Cassada Lohman, Raychelle. "Beware of the Trolls." *Psychology Today*, January 20, 2014. https://www.psychologytoday.com/blog/teen-angst/201401/beware-the-trolls.

Cassada Lohman, Raychelle. "Trolling or Cyberbullying? Or Both?" *Psychology Today*, January 28, 2014. https://www.psychologytoday.com/blog/teen-angst/201401/trolling-or-cyberbullying-or-both.

Collier, Anne. "Teens, Social Media & Trolls: Toxic Mix." Connect Safely, November 1, 2012. http://www.connectsafely.org/teens-social-media-a-trolls-toxic-mix.

Devitt, Terry. "Trolls Win: Rude Comments Dim the Allure of Science." *Wisconsin News*, February 14, 2013. http://news.wisc.edu/trolls-win-rude-comments-dim-the-allure-of-science-online.

Duggan, Maeve. "Online Harassment 2017." Pew Research Center, July 11, 2017. http://www.pewinternet.org/2017/07/11/online-harassment-2017.

Elgot, Jessica. "Cyber Self-Harm: Why Do Some Teens Troll Themselves Online." Huffington Post, October 5, 2014. http://www.huffingtonpost.co.uk/2014/05/08/cyber-self-harm_n_5288148.html.

Gammon, Jake. "Over a Quarter of Americans Have Made Malicious Online Comments." YouGov, October 20, 2014. https://today.yougov.com/news/2014/10/20/over-quarter-americans-admit-malicious-online-comm.

Get Cyber Safe. "You Think Someone You Know Is Being Cyberbullied." October 2017. https://www.getcybersafe.gc.ca/cnt/cbrbllng/tns/smn-bng-cbrblld-en.aspx.

Golbeck PhD, Jennifer. "Internet Trolls Are Narcissists, Psychopaths and Sociopaths." *Psychology Today*, September 18, 2014. https://www.psychologytoday.com/blog/your-online-secrets/201409/internet-trolls-are-narcissists-psychopaths-and-sadists.

Gordon, Sherri. "15 Ways for Bullied Kids to Take Back Their Power." Verywell.com, June 10, 2016. https://www.verywell.com/15-ways-for-bullied-kids-to-take-back-their-power-4049110.

Gordon, Sherri. "5 Times to Put an End to Rumination and Move on From Bullying." Verywell.com, June 20, 2016. https://

www.verywell.com/end-rumination-and
-bullying-460765.

Gordon, Sherri. "Life After Bullying: Learning to Be You Again." Verywell.com, February 1, 2016. https://www.verywell.com/life -after-bullying-learning-to-be-you-again -460775.

Gordon, Sherri. "What Are the Effects of Cyberbullying?" Verywell.com, August 9, 2017. https://www.verywell.com/what-are-the -effects-of-cyberbullying-460558.

Hill, Brianna. Interview with author, October 2017.

Kubota, Taylor. "Stanford Research Shows That Anyone Can Become a Troll." *Stanford News*, February 6, 2017. http://news.stanford.edu /2017/02/06/stanford-research-shows -anyone-can-become-internet-troll.

March, Evita. "Psychology of Internet Trolls: They Understand What Hurts People But Simply Don't Care." ABC News, July 13, 2017. http:// mobile.abc.net.au/news/2017-07-13/trolls -understand-what-hurts-people-but-they -simply-dont-care/8701424.

Moreau, Elise. "Internet Trolling: How Do You Spot a Real Troll?" Lifewire, June 13, 2017. https://www.lifewire.com/what-is-internet -trolling-3485891.

Rampton, John. "15 Truths About Online Trolls." *Entrepreneur*, February 17, 2015. https://www.entrepreneur.com/article/242924#.

Scheff, Sue. Interview with author, October 2017.

Sierra, Kathy. "Why Trolls Always Win." *Wired*, October 8, 2014. https://www.wired.com/2014/10/trolls-will-always-win.

Stein, Joel. "How Trolls Are Ruining the Internet." *Time*, August 18, 2016. http://time.com/4457110/internet-trolls.

Index

About the Author

Sherri Mabry Gordon is a bullying prevention advocate and author of multiple nonfiction books. Many of her books deal with issues teens face today, including bullying, abuse, public shaming, online safety, and more. Gordon also writes about bullying and patient empowerment for Verywell.com. She has given multiple presentations to schools, churches, and the YMCA on bullying prevention, dating abuse, and online safety and regularly volunteers. She also serves on the School Counselor Advisory Board for two schools. Gordon resides in Columbus, Ohio, with her husband, two children, and dog, Abbey.

Photo Credits

Cover, p. 1 Jason Stitt/Shutterstock.com; p. 5 Bloomberg /Getty Images; pp. 8, 17 Peter Dazeley/Photographer's Choice /Getty Images; p. 13 AleksandarGeorgiev/E+/Getty Images; p. 15 Brian Mitchell/Corbis/Getty Images; p. 24 DKart/iStock Unreleased /Getty Images; p. 27 kate_sept2004/E+/Getty Images; p. 30 © iStockphoto.com/Ben_Gingell; p. 34 Hero Images/Getty Images; p. 37 Mansoreh Motamedi/Moment/Getty Images; p. 40 Bill Hinton /Moment/Getty Images; p. 43 Steve Debenport/E+/Getty Images; p. 49 Kelly Sillaste/Moment Open/Getty Images; p. 51 Larry French /Getty Images Entertainment/Getty Images; pp. 52–53 Tero Vesalainen/Shutterstock.com; p. 59 Kikovic/iStock/Thinkstock; p. 63 Jamie Grill/Getty Images; p. 67 Laurence Dutton/The Image Bank /Getty Images; p. 68 © iStockphoto.com/asiseeit; p. 72 AntonioGuillem /iStock/Thinkstock; p. 75 © iStockphoto.com/Steve Debenport; p. 77 Thomas Barwick/Taxi/Getty Images; p. 79 Camerique/ClassicStock /Archive Photos/Getty Images; p. 81 Mladen Antonov/AFP /Getty Images; p. 84 Edward Carlile Portraits/Moment/Getty; p. 87 © iStockphoto.com/praetorianphoto; p. 89 Muslim Girl/DigitalVision /Getty Images; p. 92 PeopleImages/DigitalVision/Getty Images; p. 93 © iStockphoto.com/DragonImages.

Design: Nicole Russo-Duca; Layout: Ellina Litmanovich; Editor and Photo Researcher: Heather Moore Niver